ISAIAH'S SURPRISE

NANCY STELTZ

A Christmas Pageant
for the Congregation

C.S.S. Publishing Co., Inc.

Lima, Ohio

ISAIAH'S SURPRISE

7875 / ISBN 0-89536-889-7

PRINTED IN U.S.A.

Table of Contents

Characters

These two characters are to be portrayed by the same people throughout the pageant:

Isaiah   **Stage Manager**

To be able to use more people, or for a less complicated rehearsal schedule, characters such as Mary and Joseph may be portrayed by different actors in each scene.

Scene 1 — The Annunciation   Grade 8
Voice of God
Mary
Gabriel
Chorus of Voices

Scene 2 — Joseph's Quandary   Grade 9
Villagers (at least two)
Friend, male
Joseph
Angel
Narrator

Scene 3 — The Roman Decree   Grade 7
Roman Official
Villagers (at least two)
Joseph
Mary

Scene 4 — Finding a Room   Kindergarten, Grades 1 and 2
Mary
Joseph
Visitors, Beggars, Merchants (as numbers allow)
Innkeeper 1
Innkeeper 2
Innkeeper 3
Innkeeper's Wife
Children (up to seven)

Scene 5 – Jesus' Birth   Nursery, Kindergarten,
Mary   and Grade 6
Joseph
Narrators (one or two)
Reader
Speech Choir (five or more)

Scene 6 – The Shepherds   Grades 3, 4, and 5
Mary
Joseph
Shepherds (up to twelve)
Narrators (up to nine)
Angel
Host of Angels

Scene 7 – The Wise Men   Senior High
Herod
Melchior
Caspar
Balthazar
Priest
Teacher
Servant
Mary
Joseph

Prologue

Most of the classes are seated in place and some enter under the direction of the Stage Manager while the dialogue begins. Isaiah enters from the sacristy and gazes around without noticing anyone.

Isaiah: This is fascinating. I wonder where I am. And is this where the Prince of Peace will come?

(Isaiah has been walking backwards and bumps into the Stage Manager, who has been checking that everyone and everything is in the correct place.)

Isaiah: Pardon me!

Stage Manager: Oops! Excuse me. The shepherds sit over there. *(Points)*

Isaiah: Shepherds? I'm not a shepherd. My name is Isaiah; I'm a prophet.

Stage Manager *(Leafing through script)*: I don't remember a part for Isaiah here. Are you sure that's the person you're playing?

Isaiah: I'm not playing. I *am* Isaiah! — Isaiah the prophet!

Stage Manager *(Agreeing just to get things going)*: Just sit where you were told at rehearsal. We're ready to begin the Christmas pageant.

Isaiah: Christmas pageant — maybe that's it! What is this Christmas pageant about?

Stage Manager: The usual. *(Isaiah looks puzzled.)* It's about Jesus' coming to earth.

Isaiah: Could this Jesus be the Prince of Peace?

Stage Manager: Yes, he is called that, too.

Isaiah: It *is* he whose coming God foretold through me. And he's coming here now!

8

Stage Manager: You don't seem to understand. Where are you from?

Isaiah: Well, this will probably seem strange to you, but I am *the* Prophet Isaiah. *(Stage Manager looks incredulous.)* I was allowed to come to Earth to see how the Prince of Peace comes to mankind. During the reign of Uzziah, God used me to foretell the Savior's coming. I always wondered exactly how he might arrive: in a gold chariot, from white clouds, or appearing suddenly on a hill, in the forest, or *(awesomely)* in the temple?

Stage Manager: Well, it doesn't matter who you are. If you want to find out how Jesus — the Prince of Peace — came to Earth, come sit with me. We *must* begin our program now.

(Signal organist to begin; sit with Isaiah in first pew)

Opening Hymn: "Oh, Come, Oh, Come, Emmanuel" (congregation)

Isaiah: *(Stands up and looks around)* Is He coming now?

Stage Manager: *(Stands, looks where Isaiah is looking, shrugs shoulders)* Let me explain something. Our Christmas pageant tells how Jesus came to Earth almost 2,000 years ago. Now please sit down so we can go on with the program.

(Isaiah nods with some understanding; both sit down.)

Scene 1 — The Annunciation

Staging: Gabriel is on the far right; Mary is sitting center stage; the chorus stands at left stage.

Voice of God *(From microphone)*: Gabriel, you are to be my messenger to a young woman named Mary. She is engaged to Joseph, who is a descendant of Abraham and then Jesse, the father of David. Go to her in Nazareth of Galilee and tell her of the great blessing which is to be hers.

(Gabriel bows his head, then proceeds to Mary.)

Gabriel: Hail, O favored one, the Lord is with you!

Mary *(Rising)*: Wh-Who are you? What do you want?

Gabriel: Do not be afraid, Mary, for you have found favor with God. And behold, you will conceive in your womb and bear a son, and you shall call his name Jesus.

Chorus of Voices: He will be great, and will be called the Son of the Most High: and the Lord God will give to him the throne of his father David, and he will reign over the house of Jacob forever; and of his kingdom there will be no end.

Mary: How can this be, since I have no husband?

Gabriel: The Holy Spirit will come upon you, and the power of the Most High will overshadow you; therefore the child to be born will be called holy.

Gabriel and Chorus: The Son of God.

(All leave the stage.)

Isaiah *(Standing)*: I'm in the right place. This is it! — the sign God promised. *(He faces the congregation and noticeably quotes himself.)* "Therefore the Lord himself will give you a sign.

Behold, a young woman shall conceive and bear a son, and shall call his name Immanuel." . . . Immanuel — God is with us . . . I understand now. This program is preparing us for his coming. They are retelling the circumstances of his birth to set the stage for *his glorious entrance.*

Scene 2 — Joseph's Quandary

Staging: Houses are in the background; all villagers, Joseph, and Friend are on stage; the crowd is milling about and gossiping.

Villager 1: That's Joseph over there.

Villager 2: Have you heard about his betrothal?

Villager 3: She lives in Nazareth.

Villager 4: Well, I know what I would do if I were . . .

Friend: Well, Joseph, have you decided what to do about your plans for marrying Mary? From what you have told me, she is a good, kind person — and very devout. But she has put you in an awkward position.

Joseph: Mary *is* a good woman. But, under these circumstances, I cannot marry her. I've decided on a divorce — but a quiet one, of course, for her sake.

(Crowd begins to leave.)

Friend *(Nodding):* It has been a difficult decision for you to make. You look tired and it is almost dark. Go home to rest now.

(Friend and rest of villagers leave in various directions. Joseph brings out a bedroll and lies down.)

Angel *(Entering from sacristy):* Joseph, son of David, do not fear to take Mary your wife, for that which is conceived in her is of the Holy Spirit; she will bear a son, and you shall call his name Jesus, for he will save his people from their sins.

(Joseph and Angel remain in position during narration.)

Narrator: According to Matthew, chapter 1, verses 22 and 23, "All this took place to fulfill what the Lord had spoken by the prophet: 'Behold, a virgin shall conceive and bear a son, and his name shall be called Emmanuel' (which means, God with us)."

(Joseph and Angel begin to leave, stop and stare at Isaiah as he speaks)

Isaiah *(Standing up and shouting out)*: That's right! I am the prophet Matthew wrote about!

Stage Manager *(Pulling Isaiah back to his seat)*: Shhh! Please sit down and be quiet!

Scene 3 — The Roman Decree

Staging: The background of houses remains, or might be rearranged. Some people are on stage; others enter as the official begins to yell.

Roman Official *(With scroll)*: All hear this! By decree from Caesar Augustus, through Cyrenius, Governor of Syria: *All will be enrolled.* Each household will report to the birthplace of its lineage to be enrolled.

(Villagers stand around; they are commenting on the decree.)

Villager 1: That's the government for you!

Villager 2: Sure they want to count us — so they don't miss taxing someone!

Villager 3: Rome! So that's how they will keep track of us from so far away.

Villager 4: The Roman Empire, Cyrenius, Governor of Syria, the great Caesar Augustus . . .

Villager 5: They all want our money.

(Villagers leave gradually. Joseph walks toward Mary's house.)

Joseph *(Calling)*: Mary, did you hear that?

Mary *(Emerging from the house)*: Hear what, Joseph?

Joseph: The Roman government wishes to be sure that *everyone* is taxed. We must go to my ancestors' homeland to be counted.

Mary: To the city of David in Judea which is Bethlehem. It is a long journey.

Joseph: We must go. *(Both leave)*

(Rearrange the houses and add more for the Bethlehem background. The Stage Manager helps to move props and scenery. Isaiah, looking preoccupied, follows her.)

Stage Manager *(To Isaiah)*: You look as if you are trying to figure something out. What? *(Both help to arrange the stage while they are talking.)*

Isaiah *(Obviously quoting himself)*: "There shall come forth a shoot from the stump of Jesse, and a branch shall grow out of his roots."

Stage Manager: From the book of Isaiah, chapter 11, verse 1. I did my researoh for this program.

Isaiah: Yes, uh, from Isaiah. I'm trying to remember the genealogy. There was Abraham, then came his son Isaac, then Jacob, and on and on to Jesse, the father of David the king. That makes fourteen generations.

Stage Manager: Right. And then fourteen more generations until the Jews were deported to Babylon. Then thirteen more until Joseph was born. That makes Jesus the fourteenth generation again. Let's hurry; they are ready for the next scene. *(Point toward back of room)*

Scene 4 — Finding a Room

(Mary and Joseph approach from the back of the room and speak when they are halfway to the stage.)

Mary: Joseph, could that be Bethlehem just ahead?

Joseph: Yes, at last.

(Mary and Joseph continue to walk slowly toward the stage. All other Scene 4 characters take their places on stage. The visitors, beggars, and merchants yell appropriately.)

Mary: It looks so crowded.

Joseph *(Knocking on door)***:** Do you have room for us?

Innkeeper 1: There's no more room in here. This place is full because of the enrollment.

Joseph *(Knocking on second door)***:** Do you have room for us?

Innkeeper 2: None at all. I don't know of any other inn that could take you.

Joseph *(Knocking on third door)***:** Do you have any room for us?

Innkeeper 3: No. All rooms in Bethlehem are filled.

Joseph: But we have traveled all the way from Nazareth.

Mary: We are *very* tired. Please, isn't there some place for us to stay?

Innkeeper's Wife: How about the stable? At least you will be able to lie down there. I'm very busy here. Children, you can help to get the stable ready.

Child 1: I can tie the animals at one end of the stable.

Child 2: I'll put fresh hay out for you to sleep on. *(Runs off)*

Child 3: I'll put clean hay in the manger.

Child 4: I can't help; my mother told me to get right home with this.

Children 5 and 6: We'll get water from the well. You look thirsty.

Child 7: Come. I'll show you where the stable is.

(Remove scenery)

Scene 5 — Jesus' Birth

Staging: Mary, Joseph, and the baby in a manger are in center stage. The Speech Choir stands to one side.

Narrator 1: Thus it is in the small town of Bethlehem that Jesus is born to fulfill the prophet's words.

(Isaiah sits forward and listens intently.)

Reader *(Holding Bible)*: "But you, O Bethlehem Ephrathah, who are little to be among the clans of Judah, from you shall come forth for me one who is to be ruler in Israel."

Isaiah *(Standing, thinking)*: I don't recall saying — uh, reading — those words from Isaiah.

Reader *(Laughing)*: No, these are not Isaiah's words. I read from Micah, chapter 5, verse 2.

(Isaiah nods and sits down.)

Narrator 2: The birth of Jesus is told beautifully in Luke, chapter 2.

Speech Choir:

   A: "And Joseph also went up from Galilee,

   B: From the city of Nazareth,

   A and B: To Judea, to the city of David,

   All: Which is called Bethlehem,

   C: Because he was of the house and lineage of David,

   D and E: To be enrolled with Mary,

   D: His betrothed,

   E: Who was with child.

D. And while they were there, the time came for her to be delivered.

All: And she gave birth to her first-born son

E: And wrapped him in swaddling cloths,

B, C, and D: And laid him in a manger,

A: Because there was no place for them in the inn."

(Speech Choir, Narrator(s), and Reader return to their seats.)

Nursery and Kindergarten Children *(Standing next to manger scene)*: Sing "Away in the Manger"; recite a baby Jesus finger play.

Isaiah *(Standing as children are returning to their seats)*: I vividly remember my prophecy: "For to us a child is born, to us a son is given; and the government will be upon his shoulder, and his name will be called 'Wonderful Counselor, Mighty God, Everlasting Father, Prince of Peace.'" *(Isaiah approaches Mary and Joseph.)* Can you tell me — by what name was he known?

(Mary and Joseph look astonished and timid; they look to the Stage Manager for help. The Stage Manager conveys that they may answer Isaiah.)

Mary: His name is Jesus.

Joseph: It means "help of Jehovah."

Isaiah: As God's help, his Son, why was he born in such poor surroundings? A barn!

Mary: Jesus came for *all* people. His birth in a stable tells us that.

Joseph: The next couple of scenes show how God told different types of people, the rich and the poor, the educated and the illiterate, Jew and Gentile, about his Son's birth.

(Isaiah returns to his seat; he is anxious to learn more from the pageant.)

Scene 6 — The Shepherds

Staging: Mary, Joseph, and the baby in a manger are center stage. The shepherds are standing and kneeling to one far side. The Narrators hold the Bible as they are speaking.

Narrator 1: "And in that region there were shepherds out in the field, keeping watch over their flock by night."

Narrator 2: "And an angel of the Lord appeared to them, *(Angel enters from sacristy.)* and the glory of the Lord shone around them, and they were filled with fear." *(Shepherds kneel)*

Narrator 3: "And the angel said to them,

Angel *(As shepherds look up)***:** 'Be not afraid; for behold, I bring you good news of a great joy which will come to all the people; for to you is born this day in the city of David a Savior, who is Christ the Lord. And this will be a sign for you: you will find a babe wrapped in swaddling cloths and lying in a manger.

(All other angels join the Angel.)

Narrator 4: And suddenly there was with the angel a multitude of the heavenly host praising God and saying,

All Angels: 'Glory to God in the highest, and on earth peace among men with whom he is pleased!' "

(Angels sing "From Heaven Above")

Narrator 5: "When the angels went away from them into heaven, the shepherds said to one another,"

Shepherd 1: The Lord has sent us lowly shepherds many messengers.

Shepherd 2: This has to be the greatest event ever — the Savior, at last!

Shepherd 3: Let's go over to Bethlehem.

Shepherd 4: I want to see this thing that has happened.

Shepherd 5: When God has told us in this spectacular way, we *must* go.

Shepherd 6: Someone has to stay here to watch the sheep.

(General discussion about who is going, who is staying)

Shepherd 7: *(Leaving with Shepherds 8-12):* Let us see what "the Lord has made known to us."

(Shepherds 5 - 12 proceed to the stable; Shepherds 1 - 6 stay in place.)

Shepherd 8 *(Excitedly running ahead of the others):* Here is a baby in a manger.

(Shepherds 7, 9 - 12 join Shepherd 8 at the manger.)

Shepherd 9: All wrapped up in strips of cloth.

Shepherd 10 *(To Mary and Joseph):* Is this the one God told us about — Christ the Lord?

(Mary nods; the shepherds bow.)

Shepherd 11: God sent many messengers to tell us of him.

Shepherd 12: God must have great plans for this child when he grows up.

Narrator 6: After the lowly shepherds saw baby Jesus, they told others about the angels' visit and the Christ child.

(Shepherds 7 - 12 slowly walk back to Shepherds 1 - 6.)

Narrator 7: Others wondered at what the shepherds said.

Narrator 8: "But Mary kept all these things, pondering them in her heart."

(As the returning shepherds meet the others, they rejoice together.)

Narrator 9: "And the shepherds returned. glorifying and praising God for all they had heard and seen."

Shepherds' Song of Praise: "While By My Sheep"

(All leave the stage. The manger stays in place. Preparations for Scene 7 begin while Isaiah speaks.)

Isaiah *(Standing, looking around excitedly):* That was God's way of introducing his Son to the poor, uneducated people — as a baby in a stable, visited by shepherds. *(Isaiah addresses the congregation.)* Now I can hardly wait to see in what glorious array he comes to you rich, smart people.

Stage Manager *(Raising eyebrows):* Sit down!

Scene 7 — The Wise Men

Staging: Herod's court is set up to one far side. Melchior, Caspar, and Balthazar each enter from different places at the rear of the room. The Magi meet at a central place, greet each other, and look over maps and scrolls together.

Melchior: The star is still brilliant in the sky. I'm sure it will lead us to the King of the Jews.

(The three proceed toward the stage.)

Caspar: We are approaching the land of Judea.

Balthazah: King Herod is the present ruler of Judea. Surely, if the Christ child was born when the stars indicated, the king of the land will know about the event by now.

Melchior: Let's go quickly to Jerusalem to ask King Herod where the child is.

(Herod is seated in his court with his attendants. One servant leads the Magi to Herod.)

Herod: Who are you and what brings you to Jerusalem?

Melchior: We are scholars and astrologers.

Caspar: We have made a very long journey from the East. An unusual, bright star led us to this land. Our studies led us to believe that the King of the Jews has been born in your country.

Herod: *I* am King of the Jews; I reign over Judea.

Balthazar: Where is he who has been born recently to become King of the Jews, their Messiah? We saw his star in the East and have come to worship him.

Herod *(With annoyance):* I know of no such event. Now go on your way.

(The Magi bow, walk off to the opposite side, talk together, and consult the scrolls and maps again.)

Herod: *(Bellowing):* Where are the chief priests and teachers of Hebrew law? I want to see them at once! *(They enter.)*

Herod: Three wise men from the East came here looking for the Messiah. Do you know where he was to be born?

Priest: In Bethlehem of Judea; it was written by the prophet Micah.

Teacher *(Reading from scroll)*: "And you, O Bethlehem, in the land of Judah, are by no means least among the rulers of Judah; for from you shall come a ruler who will govern my people Israel."

(Herod becomes distressed, dismisses Priest and Teacher with a wave of his hand.)

Herod *(To servant)*: Find the Magi, the three wise men who came here earlier, and bring them back here. I must find out exactly when their star appeared. But don't tell anyone else about them.

(The servant bows, goes to the Magi, and returns with them. On the way, they talk and one Magi gives a scroll to the servant, who approaches Herod first.)

Servant: The Magi are here. These calculations of theirs tell what you want to know about the star.

Herod *(Looking at scroll, then speaking to Magi)*: Go and make a careful search for the child. As soon as you find him, report to me; so that I too, may go and worship him.

(The Magi bow and leave. Herod and his court leave. Mary and Joseph take their places at the manger, center stage.)

Melchior: The star is still guiding us.

(Magi walk slowly toward center stage.)

Balthazah: It seems to have stopped!

(Magi bow down at manger. Melchior hands gold to Mary.)

Mary: Gold, a gift meant for a king.

(Caspar gives frankincense to Joseph.)

Joseph *(After a subtle sniff)*: It has a very strong odor; I recall the scent of frankincense at the temple. This is a gift meant for the Son of God.

(Balthazar gives myrrh to Mary.)

Mary: Myrrh is a valuable perfume. Is its bitterness an omen of what lies ahead for this child?

(The Magi bow and exit. Mary, Joseph, and the baby in the manger remain where they are until after "What Child Is This?" *is sung. The Stage Manager is overseeing this and speaks from center stage.)*

Stage Manager *(To Isaiah especially)*: That was Christ's royal welcome to earth.

Isaiah *(Walking up to the nativity scene)*: Is that all? Isn't the mature Christ coming now — with great pageantry — to an adoring throng of people?

Stage Manager *(Standing next to Isaiah)*: I'm sorry to disappoint you with our program. You see, Jesus' ministry on earth lasted only three years, almost 2000 years ago. Sometimes throngs of people gathered around him and cheered him. However, crowds also jeered at him and hurt him.

Isaiah: As a later author of Isaiah wrote, he was "despised and rejected," "smitten and spat upon," "crucified with sinners." Two thousand years ago! Why wasn't I sent to that humble stable instead of to a play about it 2000 years later?

(Stage Manager gives Isaiah an odd look, shrugs shoulders, then goes about his/her business. Isaiah ponders a bit while looking at the nativity scene, then suddenly lights up.)

Isaiah: But that's it! The Messiah came long, long ago. And these people are still celebrating his birth 2000 years later with pageantry and joy. He is *still* the Savior for these people. *(Exit)*

Solo: "What Child Is This?" *(Sung very simply, perhaps with guitar accompaniment only)*

Offering

Benediction

Closing Hymn: "Angels from the Realms of Glory" (congregation)

About the Author

Nancy Steltz is Pastoral Assistant at Saint Paul's Lutheran Church, Trexlertown, Pennsylvania. Her responsibilities include working with the Christian Education, Social Ministry, and Youth committees and with the Lutheran Church Women and the Altar Guild. In addition, she is Volunteer Coordinator for this new mission parish. Previous to coming to Saint Paul's (in September, 1987), she served nine years as Director of Christian Education at Saint Stephen's Evangelical Lutheran Church in Allentown, Pennsylvania.

Her educational background includes a B.S. in Education, an M.Ed., and additional credits for certification. She is a certified lay professional, Level II. A member of the Evangelical Lutheran Church in America, she is included on the professional ministry roster as an Associate in Ministry.

Concerning the present publication, the author writes:

The concept of "Isaiah's Surprise" occurred to me one year as I was teaching a course about the entire Bible to the sixth-grade Sunday church school class at Trinity Lutheran Church in Bowmanstown, Pennsylvania. Years later, when we needed a Christmas pageant at Saint Stephen's, I wrote the play featuring Isaiah. "Isaiah's Surprise" focuses on just one prophet to illustrate the variety of messianic expectations that people had held at Jesus' time. In the play, Isaiah provides the link between Old Testament and New Testament. I thought the song "What Child is This?" summarized the concept of the play: Who is this paradox of lowly babe, who was born in a barn, and of unique King, who is the savior for all people? And what does it mean to me?

www.ingramcontent.com/pod-product-compliance
Lightning Source LLC
Chambersburg PA
CBHW071809020426
42331CB00008B/2453